Apples of Gold in Settings of Silver: Hidden Pictures in the Book of Ruth

APPLES OF GOLD IN SETTINGS OF SILVER: HIDDEN PICTURES IN THE BOOK OF RUTH

LORRAINE WHITE

ARPress
ILLUMINATING IDEAS
EMPOWERING VOICES

ARPress
45 Dan Road Suite 5
Canton, MA 02021

Hotline: 1(888) 821-0229
Fax: 1(508) 545-7580

Ordering Information:
Quantity sales. Special discounts are available on quantity purchases by corporations,associations, and others. For details, contact the publisher at the address above.

Printed in the United States of America.

ISBN-13:   Softcover   979-8-89356-698-7
             eBook   979-8-89356-699-4

Library of Congress Control Number: 2024904130

Contents

DEDICATION

This book is dedicated to my parents Audrey and Frank White. They have both gone on to be with the Lord but, their influence remains with all who knew them. They loved the Lord and had given themselves to Him with fullness of heart. They are greatly missed, never forgotten, and always present in spirit. I love you mom and dad.

Mom was a woman much like Ruth. She had great insight, was gentle kind and compassionate to all. She expressed God's love to others by her unselfish actions. A giver by nature, not self-gratifying but rather always looking out for the comfort and welfare of others. She stood with the Lord and His people. Nothing could or would separate her from that determination to serve and honor her heavenly Father.

Dad was a river that ran deep. He did not take the things of God lightly. He pondered over the word of God and held it close to his heart. His reverence toward the Lord exceeded the norm and he was motivated by every unction of God's Spirit and profoundly cherished His word. He honored all who walked upright before God and withdrew himself from all who held contempt toward God.

Thank you, Mom and Dad, for never giving up on me and never letting go of the righteous walk that God placed before you regardless of the many and difficult storms you had to brave.

INTRODUCTION

The phrase "apples of gold in settings of silver" comes from Proverbs 25:11,

"A word fitly spoken is like apples of gold in settings of silver."

The new covenant is hidden within the old. The new covenant messages are the apples of gold, sometimes referred to as nuggets. It is pure like gold that's been tried and fruitful in producing life. The old covenant message is the silver. It is the setting for which the new covenant is pictured, also pure and instructional. All the commandments of God are, not rules, rather they are instructions.

"I (Jesus) counsel you to buy from Me GOLD refined in the fire, that you may be rich; and white garments, that you may be clothed, that the shame of your nakedness may not be revealed and anoint your eyes with eye salve, that you may see." Revelation 13:18

"The words of the Lord are pure words, like silver tried in a furnace of earth, purified seven times." Psalms 12:6

The book of Ruth is a cherished story to every believer and even valued by non-believers as a book of inspiration. The authorship is unknown however, it is traditionally and historically accepted to be Samuel or possibly Nathan.

Ruth is known and treasured as a beautiful story of a Gentile woman who expresses her love, respect and commitment to her Hebrew mother-in-law. She becomes a proselyte of Judea and marries a relative of her deceased husband, thus bringing redemption to his name. Ruth becomes the great grandmother of king David. Therefore, she is in the lineage of the Messiah (Christ) and is listed in the record of Matthew.

"Salmon begot Boaz by Rahab, Boaz begot Obed by **Ruth**, Obed begot Jesse, and Jesse begot David the king. David the king begot Solomon by her who had been the wife of Uriah. (Mathew 1: 5&6)

The lineage continues to Yeshua (Jesus). "

"And Jacob begot Joseph the husband of Mary, of whom was born Jesus who is called Christ." (Mathew 1:16)

Many scholars believe that the word "husband", in this verse, should have been translated "father". This would certainly make sense as the lineage given here is that of Mary, whereas Luke records the lineage of Joseph her spouse. Also, because the word father is sometimes referring to a guardian as is the word husband and therefore it was probably mistranslated.

Ruth, herself, was a Moabite woman. The Moabites were heavy into idolatry, even to the extent of sacrificing their children unto their gods. The god of the Moabites was Kemosh. Therefore, the Hebrews were technically not to associate with the Moabites however, a famine in the land of Judea drove a Hebrew man, Elimelech, and, Naomi his wife, with Mahlon and Chilion, his two sons, to Moab for better living conditions.

Elimelech, Naomi's husband, dies leaving her and their two sons' left. The sons each marry a Moabite woman and they abide in Moab for about ten years then they die leaving now their mother, Naomi, with her two daughters-in-law, Orpah and Ruth.

Soon after, Naomi decides to return to her homeland, Bethlehem Judea, as she learned that they now had bread in Judea. She instructs her daughters-in-law to return to their homeland and not follow her. But to find new husbands in their own land.

Orpah chooses to return however, Ruth's heart is with Naomi her mother-in-law whom she unrelentingly clings to.

This is the point where the story begins to unfold with beautiful inspiring lessons of dedication. And although this book is primarily known for Ruth's love toward her mother-in-law and her infamous statement of commitment, there are deeper meanings and shadow pictures locked within the pages all pointing toward the new covenant and the Gentile portion of the bride of Christ.

My hope is to share with you, what has been graciously revealed to me in the reading of the book of Ruth, so that you may be enlightened with a deeper understanding, inspired, encouraged and blessed.

All Bible quotes, unless otherwise stated, are from the New King James Version. The verses of Ruth, are numbered in bold lettering to set them apart.

RUTH'S DECLARATION

"ENTREAT ME NOT TO LEAVE YOU,
OR TO TURN BACK FROM FOLLOWING
AFTER YOU;
FOR WHEREVER YOU GO, I WILL GO;
AND WHEREVER YOU LODGE, I WILL LODGE;
YOUR PEOPLE SHALL BE MY PEOPLE,
AND YOUR GOD, MY GOD.
WHERE YOU DIE, I WILL DIE,
AND THERE WILL I BE BURIED.
THE LORD DO SO TO ME, AND
MORE ALSO,
IF ANYTHING BUT DEATH PARTS YOU AND ME."

THE BOOK OF RUTH
CHAPTER 1

NEW BEGINNINGS

The time period of the judges was approximately 1100 B.C.E

1. "Now it came to pass; in the days when the judges ruled, that there was a famine in the land. And a certain man of Bethlehem, Judah, went to dwell in the country of Moab, he and his wife and his two sons."

The word of God is not put together by happenstance. There is always a reason for the things written. We learn from the statement "in the days when the judges ruled", that there is a correlation in the book of Ruth showing that the shadow or picture type of the book is pointing to the Gentile segment of the Bride of Christ. Because in the book of judges, we read of twelve men and one woman who judge Israel. This is a type of the twelve apostles (representing the twelve tribes, the twelve male judges) and the bride of Christ (representing the body/church of Christ, the one female judge) who will rule and reign with Him during the last thousand years.

"So, Jesus said to them, 'Assuredly I say to you, that in the regeneration, when the Son of Man sits on the throne of His Glory, you who have

1

followed me will also sit on twelve thrones, judging the twelve tribes of Israel." (Math 19:28) Here Jesus is talking to His 12 apostles.

"Do you not know that we shall judge angels? How much more, things that pertain to this life?" (1 Cor 6:3) Here the apostle Paul is addressing the Corinthian assembly.

2. **"The name of the man was Elimelech, the name of his wife was Naomi, and the names of his two sons were Mahlon and Chilion----Ephrathites of Bethlehem, Judah. And they were in the country of Moab and remained there. "**

Names, in the bible, denote a nature or reveal a specific characteristic. Learning the etymology and meaning of a bible name can give you a clearer insight into the message being delivered.

They were Ephrathites. Ephraath is another word for Bethlehem.

Ephraath or Ephrathah; from 'parah', (6509) fruitfulness; Ephrath, another name for Bethlehem. (Strong's H672)

Bethlehem means house of bread. It is the birthplace of the Messiah. That "spiritual" bread brought down from heaven, that is, the word of God."

Beyth Lechem, from 'bayith' (1004) and 'lechem' (3899); house of bread" (Strong's H1035)

"But you, Bethlehem, Ephrathah, though you are little among the thousands of Judah, Yet, out of you shall come forth to Me the One to be Ruler in Israel, whose goings forth are from old, from everlasting." (Micah 5:2)

"In the beginning was the word, and the word was with God, and the word was God." (John 1:1)

"And the word became flesh and dwelt among us, and we beheld His glory, the glory as of the only begotten of the Father, full of grace and truth." (John 1:14)

"Then Jesus said to them, 'Most assuredly, I say to you; Moses did not give you the bread from heaven, but My Father gives you the true bread from heaven." (John 6:32)

"For the bread of God is He who comes down from heaven and gives life to the world." (John 6:33)

"Then they said to Him, 'Lord, give us this bread always." (John 6: 34)

"And Jesus said to them, 'I am the bread of life. He who comes to Me shall never hunger, and he who believes in me shall never thirst." (John 35)

Judah is of great significance because the Messiah was to be of the tribe of Judah and a descendant of king David, who is also of Judah.

"The scepter shall not depart from Judah, nor a lawgiver from between his feet, until Shiloh comes; And to Him shall be the obedience of the people" (Gen 49:10)

"There shall come forth a Rod out of the stem of Jesse, and a Branch shall grow out of his roots." (Isaiah 11:1)

"Hear oh Joshua, the high priest, you and your companions who sit before you, for they are a wondrous sign; for behold, I am bringing forth My Servant the BRANCH." (Zechariah 3:8)

"I, Jesus, have sent My angel to testify to you these things in the churches. I am the Root and the Offspring of David, the Bright and Morning Star." (Revelation 22:16)

Elimelech – God is King. The meaning of Elimelech lets us know that, God is in control of all, as ruler and supreme judge, He orders our steps. Therefore, the biblical occurrences, historic, present or future, are not mere circumstance but planed and presented by Jehovah himself.

El – strength; as adj. mighty; especially the Almighty (but used also of any deity): God (god) – Strong's H410

Melech -king – melek from 4427; a king- king, royal – Strong's H4428

Naomi – Pleasant. The meaning of Naomi reveals that, she was a woman of gratification and agreeable, (not argumentative) and enjoyable, or a pleasure to be around.

Naomi is representative of the Hebrew body of Christ, the mother of the Gentiles. She takes in the Gentile and embraces them with a mother's love.

"Rejoice with Jerusalem, and be glad with her, all you who love her; Rejoice for joy with her, all you who mourn for her;

"That you may feed and be satisfied with the consolation of her bosom, that you may drink deeply and be delighted with the abundance of her glory."

"For thus says the LORD: 'Behold, I will extend peace to her like a river; And the glory of the Gentiles like a flowing stream, then you shall feed; On her sides shall you be carried, and be dandled on her knees"

"As one whom his mother comforts, so I will comfort you; And you shall be comforted in Jerusalem." (Isaiah 66: 1-12)

It was the Apostle Peter who, being commissioned by the Lord, brought the gospel to the Gentiles (others came with him). Beginning with a man named Cornelius who had fasted and prayed to the God of Abraham, and the many that were with him. All of them being Gentiles.

"While Peter was still speaking these words, the Holy Spirit fell upon all those who heard the word."

" And those of the circumcision who believed were astonished, as many as came with Peter, because the gift of the Holy Spirit had been poured out on the Gentiles also."

"For they heard them speak with tongues and magnify God. Then Peter answered,"

"Can anyone forbid water, that these should not be baptized who have received the Holy Spirit just as we have?"

"And he commanded them to be baptized in the name of the Lord. Then they asked him to stay a few days." (Acts 10: 44-48}

Although Naomi represents the church bringing the Gentiles into the inheritance of Abraham, Sarah, Abraham's wife, represents the mother of the entire body of Christ. She is the "free woman".

"For it is written that Abraham had two sons: the one by a bondwoman, the other by a freewoman through promise,"

"which things are symbolic. For these are the two covenants: the one from Mount Sinai which gives birth to bondage, which is Hagar"

"for this Hagar is Mount Sinai in Arabia, and corresponds to Jerusalem which now is, and is in bondage with her children"

"but the Jerusalem above is free, which is the mother of us all."

"For it is written:

'Rejoice, O barren, you who do not bear! Break forth and shout, you who are not in labor! For the desolate has many more children than she who has a husband."

"Now we, brethren, as Isaac was, are children of promise."

"But, as he who was born according to the flesh then persecuted him who was born according to the Spirit, even so it is now."

"Nevertheless, what does the scripture say? 'Cast out the bondwoman and her son, for the son of the bondwoman shall not be heir with the son of the freewoman."

"So then, brethren, we are not children of the bondwoman but of the free." (Galatians 4:22-31}

Mahlon – Sickly/weak. Chilion – pining. The name Mahlon informs us that he was not simply physically weak or sickly but weak in character and lacking spiritual strength. He represented the dead works approach to the law and weak in faith toward God. While Chilion is a type of the Israel who not seeing God in the scriptures, cling desperately to their traditions while it is pining away.

"For what the law could not do in that it was **weak through the flesh**, God did by sending His own Son in the likeness of sinful flesh, on account of sin: He condemned sin in the flesh,"

"that the righteous requirements of the law might be fulfilled in us who do not walk according to the flesh but according to the Spirit." (Romans 8: 3-4)

They are a type of the old covenant and the religious element of Israel.

"My little children, for whom I labor in birth again until Christ is formed in you,"

"I would like to be present with you now and to change my tone; for I have doubts about you."

"Tell me, you who desire to be under the law, do you not hear the law?" (Galatians 4:19-21)

The law which could not be replaced but fulfilled through Christ through the strength of the covenant.

"Then I will give them one heart, and I will put a new spirit within them; and take the stony heart out of their flesh, and give them a heart of flesh," (Ezekiel 11:19)

"That they may walk in My statutes and keep My judgments and do them; and they shall be My people, and I will be their God." (Ezekiel 11:20)

"Behold the days are coming, says the LORD, when I will make a new covenant with the house of Israel and with the house of Judah" -----

"Not according to the covenant that I made with their fathers in the day that I took them by the hand to lead them out of the land of Egypt, M2y covenant which they broke, though I was a husband to them, says the LORD."

"But this is the covenant that I will make with the house of Israel after those days, says the LORD: I will put My law in their minds, and write it on their hearts; and I will be their God, and they shall be My people." (Jeremiah 31:31-33)

3. **"Then Elimelech, Naomi's husband, died; and she was left, and her two sons."**
4. **"Now they took wives of the women of Moab: the name of the one was Orpah, and the name of the other Ruth. And they dwelt there about ten years."**

Women in the bible frequently will represent churches or assemblies of people including cities. Therefore, in this passage the marriage of these two Gentile women depicts the union of the Gentile church with Jerusalem, Judah.

"For I am jealous for you with a godly jealousy. For I have betrothed you to one husband, that I may present you as a chaste virgin to Christ." (2Corinthians 11:2)

"John answered and said, 'A man can receive nothing unless it has been given to him from heaven."

"You yourselves bear me witness, that I said, 'I am not the Christ', but I have been sent before Him."

"He who has the bride is the bridegroom; but the friend of the bridegroom, who stands and hears him, rejoices greatly because of the bridegroom's voice. Therefore, this joy of mine is fulfilled." (John 3: 27-29)

"Their names: Oholah the elder and Oholibah her sister; They were Mine, and they bore sons and daughters. As for their names Samaria is Oholah, and Jerusalem is Oholibah." (Ezekiel 23:4)

"Then I John saw the holy city, New Jerusalem, coming down out of heaven from God, prepared as a bride adorned for her husband." (Revelation 21:2)

"And I heard a loud voice from heaven saying, 'Behold the tabernacle of God is with men, and He will dwell with them, and they shall be His people. God Himself will be with them and be their God." (Revelation 21:3)

Referring to verse 4, Naomi stays on with her sons and their wives for a period of 10 years prior to their death.

The number 10 in the bible often depicts a time of proofing and completion. Thus, when the time was completed, the love and commitment that these two Gentile women had toward Naomi would be proved.

Examples of 10 being used are:

The 10 plagues God brought on Egypt, which tested Pharaoh and the Egyptians and esteemed His name above the gods of Egypt's.

In order they were:

1. Turning the Nile to blood, rendering it full of dead fish and undrinkable. (Hapi - god of the Nile)
2. Horrific multitudes of frogs both over the land and in the homes. (Heckel – goddess of frogs.)
3. Un relenting lice on men and animals. (Geb – god of earth. The lice emerged from the dust of the earth.)
4. An infestation of flies throughout all of Egypt. (Kepri – god of creation. Had the head of a fly.)

5. Great pestilence upon the livestock, causing many to die. (Hathor – god of love and protection. Commonly depicted with the head of a cow.)

6. Boils upon both men and beast causing intense misery. (Isis – goddess of medication and peace.)

7. Large hail stones dropped, killing any living thing in the fields, including vegetation. (Nut – goddess of sky. It rained hail and fire)

8. Thick clouds of locusts swarming in and consuming vegetation left from the hail. (Seth – god of storms and disorder. The locusts blackened the sky.)

9. An eerie, thick, total darkness over the land whereby no one could function for the lack of sight. (Ra – the son god. Three days of darkness.)

10. And finally, that which caused Pharaoh to relent whereby God instituted the Pass Over, was the killing of the first born of both men and animal. (Pharaoh - primary god. The Pharaoh was considered the resolute god with power and decisiveness and regarded as the most majestic of all the gods.)
(Exodus 7 – 12)

The 10 commandments given to be a proofing of mankind's will and desire towards their creator to do and keep His word in their hearts making them complete or perfect before God.

1. I am the LORD your God, you shall not have any other gods before me….

2. You shall not make for yourself a carved image….

3. You shall not take the name of the LORD your God in vain….

4. Remember the Sabbath day, to keep it holy….

5. Honor your father and your mother….

6. You shall not murder.

7. You shall not commit adultery.

8. You shall not steal.

9. You shall not bare false witness against your neighbor.
10. You shall not covet.... (Ex 20:1-17)

5. "Then Mahlon and Chilion also died; so, the woman survived her two sons and her husband."

The demise of Mahlon and Chilion, is a type of the demise of "old" Israel which had become weak and sickly in the things of God. The transition leading to the demise of "old" Israel, began with the coming of Christ and was completed with the siege, annihilation, and dispersion by Titus and his Roman army about 70 c. e.

6. "Then she arose with her daughters-in-law that she might return from the country of Moab, for she had heard in the country of Moab that the LORD had visited His people by giving them bread."

7. "Therefore, she went out from the place where she was, and her two daughters-in-law with her, and they went on their way to return to the land of Judah."

Here we see a picture of the true Jerusalem, being called to return to the land of bread. That is turn to the bread of life and truth of God, and accompanying her are the Gentile believers.

8. "And Naomi said to her two daughters-in-law, 'Go, return each to her mother's house. The LORD deal kindly with you, as you have with the dead and with me."

9. "The LORD grant that you may find rest, each in the house of her husband." So she kissed them, and they lifted up their voices and wept.

10. "And they said to her, surely we will return with you to your people."

11. "But Naomi said, 'Turn back, my daughters; why will you go with me? Are there still sons in my womb, that they may be your husbands?"

12. "Turn back, my daughters, go-for I am too old to have a husband. If I should say I have hope, if I should have a husband tonight and should also bear sons"

13. "would you wait for them till they were grown? Would you restrain yourselves from having husbands? No, my daughters; for it grieves me very much for your sakes that the hand of the LORD has gone out against me!"

Naomi's love and commitment and that of the two daughters-in-law toward Naomi and her people whom they married into are tested and proved.

Placed before them is the opportunity to return to their mother's house and their former religion, where things are familiar and they can find comfort and rest, or to continue on and become allotted with Judah and an heir of Abraham.

Naomi reveals her tenderness and unselfishness by giving blessings and well wishes without demanding loyalty although she is disturbed within herself thinking the LORD has gone against her in that she has lost her husband and sons.

"I tell the truth in Christ, I am not lying, my conscience also bearing me witness in the Holy Spirit,"

"That I have great sorrow and continual grief in my heart."

"For I could wish that I myself were accursed from Christ for my brethren, my countrymen according to the flesh." (Rom 9: 1-3)

14. "Then they lifted up their voices and wept again; and Orpah kissed her mother-in-law, but Ruth clung to her."

15. "And she said, 'Look, your sister-in-law has gone back to her people and to her gods; return after your sister-in-law."

16. "But Ruth said:"

"Entreat me not to leave you, or to turn back from following after you; For wherever you go, I will go; And wherever you lodge, I will lodge; Your people will be my people, And your God my God."

17. "Where you die, I will die, and there will I be buried, The LORD do so to me, and more also, If anything but death parts you and me."

Verses 16 and 17 have become one of the most famous verses of the bible. They are used as examples of commitment in congregations around the globe. The depth of love and devotion Ruth has exhibits unparalleled veneration. She had priorly determined to commit her life to the God of Israel and His people and would not be deterred.

This is a foreshadowing of the two elements of the Gentile church. The one, Orpah, turns away from the truth and returns to her familiar gods and religious ways. Rather than transitioning to "The House of Bread" she returns to the comfort of her former house of idolatry. The New Testament writings records the church falling away and returning to her former ways. The apostles were very aware of the falling away and warned the church but not all had an ear to hear.

"For I know this, that after my departure savage wolves will come in among you, not sparing the flock."

"Also, from among yourselves men will rise up, speaking perverse things, to draw away the disciples after themselves."

"Therefore watch, and remember that for three years I did not cease to warn everyone night and day with tears." (Acts 20:29-31)

John writes in his epistle to Gaius, (The third epistle) that he and his fellow companions were not even being received by a Gentile church.

"I wrote to the church, but Diotrephes, who loves to have the preeminence among them, does not receive us."

"Therefore, if I come, I will call to mind his deeds which he does, prating against us with malicious words. And not content with that, he himself does not receive the brethren, and forbids those who wish to, putting them out of the church." (Third John 1: 9-10)

"But the Jerusalem above is free, which is the mother of us all." (Gal 4:26)

The greater majority of the Gentile church slipped back to their religions and incorporated the practices, beliefs and gods into the church. Today they are so mingled in, it's difficult to separate the truth from falsehood. Yet there was always a portion that would not bow their knee to the idolatry that was finding its way into the church and they, for the most part, were persecuted for their non-conformity. They were the Ruth's who committed themselves to the God of Abraham, Isaac and Jacob and became a daughter to the true Jerusalem.

The greater majority turned back to the comfort of paganism in a very subtle way. Like Orpah, who had no doubt grieved the loss of her husband and upon hearing the prospect of having a new husband, turned and went back to her gods. So was the church grieved through persecution and was therefore easily lulled into accepting the promise of peace through Constantine's edicts and religious structure. History teaches that Constantine worshipped the Sun deity named Invictus/ Mithra/Apollo; who was born on Dec. 25th. These all were other names of Tammuz or Baal the sun god. Constantine wanted to unify Rome and a means to do so was through the unification of religion. He made a decree of Sun-day as the day of rest to replace the Sabbath in 321 c. e. He despised the Jews as they would not conform and therefore, would not tolerate any "Jewish custom" brought into Rome. He pillaged all the pagan temples and confiscated the pagan statues where he erected them as Christian saints. For example, the Statues of St. Peter at Vatican City and in the Basilica were originally a statue of Jupiter or as some believe, Zeus. Although, a very few were constructed in intervals up to around the 14th century the majority are from the Constantine era. He placed the pillaged statues throughout Constantinople at various place throughout Rome's empire to represent his new gods.

In 325 C.E. the council of Nicaea was held and Pagan Bishops of polytheism came to discuss how to establish a date for Easter (the same as the goddess Ishtar, mother of Tammuz) and also, the doctrine of the trinity. They were to develop a new god for the purpose of unification among the people of the Roman Empire. The delegates argued amongst themselves and brought in the characteristics of their own gods. There were 53 gods in total that were brought to the table for debate. (Ref. God's Book of Eskra, Prof. S.L. MacGuire's translation, Salisbury, 1922, chapter 48 pg.36, 41)

Constantine, who was not particularly interested in the Nicaea meeting, had resumed his leadership activities and after 1 ½ years of the debating he returned to find that they had narrowed their new god down to: 1. Caesar 2. Krishna 3. Mithra 4. Horus and 5. Zeus. (Historia Ecclesiastica, Eusebius, c, 325).

Because Constantine was emperor, he made the decision of which would be the god and because he perceived Christ as a re-incarnated Tammuz, he chose his god Mithra but called him the Latin Iesus from the Greek Ieosus, which was adopted because there was no J in the Hebrew ABaRiY/Negro alphabet they were using they did not properly translate the name Joshua or rather (J)Yahushua the letter J making a Y sound. The English Jesus is thus from the Greek and Latin translations.

His adaptation of the god Mithra was well received and not refuted by the general populace. Those that disagreed with his decrees faced severe consequences including flogging, torture and execution. The gods and goddesses of travel, birth, agriculture, weather, rivers and even sewers etc. were declared to be "Saints" (a mini god of sorts, that one can pray to) by church authority and the word saint was taken away from the defining of a believer and follower of Christ.

At the counsel of Nicaea, the Passover was replaced with Easter, sun worship via the sun god's and goddesses was brought in with disguise, and the idea of a tri-god was brought to the forefront however, not established as church doctrine until 381 c. e. when the second church meeting convened in Constantinople by the summoning of emperor Theodosius. (This church doctrine became so engrained that some individuals worship the spirit of God more than God himself. As an example, a popular song was written by Reginald Heber called "Holy, Holy, Holy" with the ending stanza, a verse; "God in three persons, blessed trinity".) Had a person gone into one of the early first century assemblies using the term "blessed trinity", no one would have known what they were talking about as it simply didn't exist. Also, they would never have replaced Passover with Ishtar or Easter neither would they have assigned a false birth date to our Lord in order to continue in the worship of their sun-gods. Jesus did not teach such things, neither did the apostles. It took 300 years of *not* contending for the faith first delivered to the saints (believers) to create these doctrines and more years to force them to acceptance. Verses are twisted to fit the narrative.

"as also in all his (Paul's) epistles, speaking in them of these things, in which are some things hard to understand, which untaught and unstable people twist to their own destruction, as they do also the rest of the scriptures." (2 Peter 3:16)

Constantine, in 313 c. e., after the battle of Milvian Bridge where he was victorious and saw a cross image in the sky with the words "In this Sign you will Conquer, gave an edict from himself and emperor Licinius, which proclaimed religious tolerance throughout all of Rome. This edict stopped the persecution of Christians and Constantine because of his victory and the sign made Christianity the religion of the Roman Empire. He then, using that sign like a banner, went out with his armies to conquer the people and force them to accept the religious governing of Rome.

The church had been at different times light persecution and at other times heavy persecution, especially when the emperors Diocletian, Maximus, Galarius and Constantias governed. The majority of Christians relented to the safety of Rome's covering and many had forgotten the "true way". They turned their back on Jerusalem above and embraced again their familiar gods; presented as Christian saints. They became Orpah's who kissed their mother-in-law goodbye forever, and the Ruth's became the woman, who was hidden in Christ, nourished and preserved by our Heavenly Father.

Rev. 12:14 "But the woman was given two wings of a great eagle, that she might fly into the wilderness to her place, where she is nourished for a time and times and half a time, from the presence of the serpent."

18. **"When she saw that she was determined to go with her, she stopped speaking to her."**

She didn't quit talking to her but rather, she dropped the subject and didn't press it any further.

19. **"Now the two of them went until they came to Bethlehem. And it happened, when they had come to Bethlehem, that all the city was excited because of them; and the women said, 'Is this Naomi?"**
20. **"But she said to them, 'Do not call me Naomi; call me Mara, for the Almighty has dealt very bitterly with me."**
21 **"I went out full, and the LORD has brought me home again empty. Why do you call me Naomi, since the LORD has testified against me, and the Almighty has afflicted me?"**

It's apparent the Naomi was a well-known woman of the community as they all were excited to see her. But Naomi was still hurting from her loss of husband and two sons and therefore responds with, 'call me Mara for I am bitter as I went out full and now am empty." That is, she felt full within herself but, she now feels empty within herself.

The word Mara means bitter. The first time we see the word is when the Israelites during their exodus from Egypt happen upon a place named Mara.

"So, Moses brought Israel from the Red Sea; then they went out into the Wilderness of Shur. And they went three days in the wilderness and found no water."
"Now when they came to Marah, they could not drink the waters of Marah, for they were bitter. Therefore, the name of it was called Marah." (Ex 15: 22-

The difference in spelling is a result of the difference in time and language use.

Jerusalem was thrust from her land and into that of the Gentiles when the Roman army under the command of Titus invaded, defeated, and dispersed them. She'd lost her husband and sons. Her entire religious, political, and economical system was now destroyed. The Jerusalem of "old" was now forever gone.

But she has returned and is still returning. The Jews begin migrating back to their homeland in the late 1800's and early 1900's.

On November 2, 1917, through the persuasion of Chaim Weizmann a Zionist statesperson, a statement was written by Arthur James Balfour to the British foreign secretary, stating the support of Britain to establish a national homeland in Palestine for the Jewish people and was delivered to Lionel Walter Rothchild, a profound leader in the Anglo-Jewish community. This now is known as the "Balfour Declaration" and it was supported by Woodrow Wilson, then residing president of the United States. The Jews had given support to the British against the Turks during World War 1 and thus the League of Nations sanctioned the declaration and assigned Britain to rule the Palestine territory.

While the ground work was being prepped for the establishment of a Jewish state, there were many Jews migrating to their homeland. Their return is termed "Aliyah". The first Aliyah was in the late 1800's, mostly from Russia and Yemen. The second Aliyah was prior to Word War 1 and was made up of Russian Jews. They began the first Kibbutz and are responsible for reviving the Hebrew language. From the end of World War 1 and up until 1923 was the third Aliyah, also from Russia. The fourth Aliyah around 1924 – 1929 was made up of a variety of Jewish persons escaping the anti-Semitic nations they resided in. There has since been a continual influx of Jews to Israel who are seeking to re-unite with their homeland.

From 1933 to 1945 the Hebrew nation went through an onslaught of abusive hatred instigated by the officials of Germany, namely Hitler and his regime. The intent to finger out and alienate all the Jews to extreme and vile, mind boggling measures of persecution, up to and including execution right under the nose of the entire world is incomprehensible. Yet, that is exactly what happened. The "Holocaust" became the major theme of World War 11, and catapulted every able and wanting Jew to their homeland.

The United States and Britain made a joint effort to establish the "Anglo-American Committee of Inquiry" and in April of 1946 the committee had furnished ten suggestions, titled, "The Avalon Project" which included in its topics "The need for peace in Palestine". Reactions to the suggestions were unfavorable by Arabs Jews and British. By 1947 the communication between the Arabs and Jews had disintegrated. Resulting was the British becoming anxious to rid itself of its mandate over Palestine and the wheels were set in motion for the U.N. General Assembly to set up a "Special Committee on Palestine (UNSCOP), recommending that the mandate of the British over Palestine be ended and the land be divided into two states. This set off a chain of mixed reactions. In the interim the then residing President Truman instructed the State Department to support the U.N. plan, for which it complied with hesitancy. In 1948 with the authoritative aid of the United States and Great Britain, they became a recognized nation and Israel was put on the map.

"At midnight on May 14,1948, the Provisional Government of Israel proclaimed a new State of Israel. On that same date, the United States, in the person of President Truman, recognized the provisional Jewish government as de facto authority of the Jewish state." (de jure recognition was extended on January 31, 1949)

(Press release is from the records of Charles G. Ross Alphabetical File, other information is obtained from the records of the Department of State, Record Group 59, National Archives and Records Administration, Washington DC.)

The Jews have returned and it has been bitter-sweet. Six million of theirbrethren were killed during the Holocaust. About a third of their worldwide population. To return for some meant a long hard journey of trekking on foot. Going hungry, cold and exhausted yet, the spirit within remained strong and egged them on toward their reward where they've met opposition and have had to remain in constant military conflict to maintain what little ground they've gained. (**But she said to them, 'Do not call me Naomi; call me Mara, for the Almighty has dealt very bitterly with me."**

"I went out full, and the LORD has brought me home again empty. Why do you call me Naomi, since the LORD has testified against me, and the Almighty has afflicted me?")

22. "So Naomi returned, and Ruth the Moabitess her daughter-in-law with her, who returned from the country of Moab. Now they came to Bethlehem at the beginning of barley harvest."

Barley harvest is the time of the Pass Over. The harvesters were gathering in the barley from the fields while at home they were ensuring that all leaven was removed. There was to be no leaven to be within the city.

"For I shall pass through the land of Egypt on that night, and will strike all the firstborn in the land of Egypt both man and beast; and against all the gods of Egypt I will execute judgment: I am the LORD."

"Now the blood shall be a sign for you on the houses where you are. And when I see the blood, I will pass over you; and the plague shall not be on you to destroy you when I strike the land of Egypt."

"So this day shall be to you a memorial; and you shall keep it as a feast to the LORD throughout your generations. You shall keep it as a feast by an everlasting ordinance."

"Seven days you shall eat unleavened bread. On the first day you shall remove leaven from your houses. For whoever eats leavened bread from the first day until the seventh day, that person shall be cut off from Israel." (Exodus 12: 12-15)

"For seven days no leaven shall be found in your houses, since whoever eats what is leavened, that same person shall be cut off from the congregation of Israel, whether he is a stranger or a native of the land."

"You shall eat nothing leavened; in all your dwellings you shall eat unleavened bread." (Exodus 12: 19-20)

Leaven in the Bible is a type of sin or false doctrine.

"Therefore, purge out the old leaven, that you may be a new lump, since you truly are unleavened. For indeed Christ, our Passover, was sacrificed for us. (1Cor 5:7)

The arrangements of God are always on time. Ruth and Naomi arrive in Bethlehem, Judah at the time of the preparation of the Passover. Coinciding with Christ, our Passover, which His crucifixion opened the door for the Gentiles salvation that they might be a part of His beautiful bride and His glorious body.

"For God so loved the ***world*** that He gave His only begotten Son, that whoever believes on Him should not parish but have everlasting life." (John 3:16)

The word world is from G2889 – Kosmos, which refers to an orderly arrangement or universe or of course, our entire earth-world.

G165 is the Greek word aion or English eon which would be referring to the era or the age, a space of time.

With this understanding we know that He died, was buried and resurrected for the salvation of **all** mankind.

THE BOOK OF RUTH

CHAPTER 2

1. **"There was a relative of Naomi's husband, a man of great wealth, of the family of Elimelech. His name was Boaz."**

Boaz is often termed as "swiftness". In the Hebrew however, it means "strength is in him". Also, the coming goat. Thus, pointing directly to Christ. Boaz is therefor, represented as a type of the Messiah. He foreshadows Christ and His redemption of the Gentile.

2. **"So Ruth the Moabitess said to Naomi, 'Please let me go to the field, and glean heads of grain after him in whose sight I may find favor.' And she said to her, 'Go my daughter."**

Ruth knew the law of the land, that she, as a stranger in Israel, would be given the privilege of gleaning. Her desire to work in the field and supply their table with bread is lauded and worthy of praise. She is those early Gentle believers who had a hunger and eagerness to reap in all they could from the word of God.

3. **"Then she left, and went and gleaned in the field after the reapers. And she happened to come to the part of the field belonging to Boaz, who was of the family of Elimelech."**

4. **"Now behold, Boaz came from Bethlehem, and said to the reapers, 'The LORD be with you!' And they answered him, 'The LORD bless you!"**

Boaz, like the Messiah, comes from Bethlehem, the house of bread. He is in the family of Elimelech, Ruth's deceased father-in-law, thus a near kinsman to Ruth's deceased husband.

This is important because Jehovah had established the law of redemption for a widow by a near kinsman. He foreshadows Christ as a redeemer for all Gentile believers along with the Jewish believers.

5. **"Then Boaz said to his servant who was in charge of the reapers, 'Whose young woman is this?"**
6. **"So the servant who was in charge of the reapers answered and said, 'It is the young Moabite woman who came back with Naomi from the country of Moab."**
7. **"And she said 'Please let me glean and gather after the reapers among the sheaves.' So she came and has continued from morning until now though she rested a little in the house."**
8. **"Then Boaz said to Ruth, 'You will listen, my daughter, will you not? Do not go to glean in another field, nor go from here, but stay close by my young women."**

"You will listen, my daughter, will you not?" This is much like "Hear O Israel". The word "listen" is the same word used for "hear", in the Hebrew. (Strong's # H8035 -Shama, or can be spelled Shema, meaning to hear intelligently (often with implication of attention, obedience, etc.) It is therefore, literally implying to pay attention and do as is stated.

She is instructed to not glean in another field. Likewise, Christ's church is not to glean in another field. We need to be reaping and gleaning from His word only. We need to stay close to Him and His people.

9. **"Let your eyes be on the field which they reap, and go after them Have I not commanded the young men not to touch**

you? And when you are thirsty, go to the vessels and drink from what the young men have drawn."

This is comparable to the early beginnings of the Gentile entry into the field of God. The young men, in this setting, would be representative of the apostles and Jewish brethren. "Now the apostles and brethren who were in Judea heard that the Gentiles had also received the word of God."

"And when Peter came up to Jerusalem, those of the circumcision contended with him,"

"Saying, 'You went in to uncircumcised men and ate with them!"

"But Peter explained it to them in order from the beginning, saying;"

"I was in the city of Joppa praying; and in a trance I saw a vision, an object descending like a great sheet, let down from heaven by four corners; and it came to me."

"When I observed it intently and considered, I saw four footed animals of the earth, wild beasts, creeping things, and birds of the air."

"And I heard a voice saying to me, 'Rise. Peter; kill and eat."

"But I said, 'Not so, Lord! For nothing common or unclean has at any time entered my mouth."

"But the voice answered me again from heaven, 'What God has cleansed you must not call common."

"Now this was done three times, and all were drawn up again into heaven.

"At that very moment, three men stood before the house where I was, having been sent to me from Caesarea."

"Then the Spirit told me to go with them, doubting nothing. Moreover, these six brethren accompanied me, and we entered the man's house."

"And he told us how he had seen an angel standing in his house, who said to him, 'Send men to Joppa, and call for Simon whose surname is Peter,"

"who will tell you words by which you and all your household will be saved."

"And as I began to speak, the Holy Spirit fell upon them, as upon us at the beginning."

"Then I remembered the word of the Lord, how He said, 'John indeed baptized with water; but you shall be baptized with the Holy Spirit."

"If therefore God gave them the same gift as He gave us when we believed on the Lord Jesus Christ, who was I that I could withstand God?"

"When they heard these things, they became silent; and they glorified God, saying, 'Then God has also granted to the Gentiles repentance to life." (Acts 11: 1-18)

10. "So she fell on her face, bowed down to the ground, and said to him, 'Why have I found favor in your eyes, that you should take notice of me, since I am a foreigner?"

The same is in the heart of the believer, who recognizes the grace of God to touch their lives and receive them into His fold. Especially those early Gentile believers who did not even know the God of Abraham and had no inheritance until Christ.

News of Naomi and Ruth had spread throughout Bethlehem and Boaz knew of Ruth's ethics and candor, and that she was considered a virtuous woman. Thus, Boaz showed favor toward her and honored the labor she put forth in his field just as Christ takes notice and favors every Gentile believer who hungers enough for the things of God to labor in His field and gather all he can.

11. "And Boaz answered and said to her, 'It has been fully reported to me, all that you have done for your mother-in-law since the death of your husband, and how you have left your father and your mother and the land of your birth, and have come to a people whom you did not know before."

12. "The LORD repay your work, and a full reward be given you by the LORD God of Israel, under whose wings you have come for refuge."

Ruth displayed the aspiration of the true believer whom Christ spoke of as being those who'd receive eternal life.

"And everyone who has left houses or brothers or sisters or father or mother or wife or children or lands, for My name's sake, shall receive a hundredfold, and inherit eternal life." (Matt 19:29)

To come under God's wings is to come before His mercy and His covering. In the tabernacle's Holy of Holies or Most Holy was the ark with the covenant and the "mercy" seat was over it and the two Cherubim's Covered it with their wings.

13. "Then she said, 'Let me find favor in your sight, my lord; for you have comforted me, and have spoken kindly to your maidservant, though I am not like one of your maidservants."

14. "Now Boaz said to her at mealtime, 'Come here, and eat of the bread, and dip your piece of bread in the vinegar.' So she sat beside the reapers, and he passed parched grain to her; and she ate and was satisfied, and kept some back."

The term "come here" insinuates to the throne "and eat some bread" is the bread of the throne. "And dip your bread in the vinegar" refers to the suffering of our LORD. (Theological Dictionary of Rabbinic Judaism pg. 161)

When he passed parched grain to her it was what he had pinched between his fingers and passed to her. (Theological Dictionary of Rabbinic Judaism pg.163)

This interpretation would coincide with the fact that it was Passover time which is a feast or appointed time that is aimed toward Christ, the bread from heaven and the suffering price He paid so we through Him are able to approach the throne of our Father. At the last supper Christ broke bread and passed it to His disciples.
"And as they were eating, Jesus took bread, blessed and broke it, and gave it to the disciples and said, "Take, eat; this is my body" (Matt 26:26)

15. "And when she rose up to glean, Boaz commanded his young men, saying, 'Let her glean even among the sheaves, and do not reproach her."
16. "Also let grain from the bundles fall purposely for her; leave it that she may glean, and do not rebuke her."

Boaz like Christ, puts up a hedge of protection for Ruth and gives the word that she is to freely glean the field without reproach even that they should purposely allow grain to fall for her to gather. Further she was allowed to enter in amongst the sheaves. She therefore was not viewed as a stranger or an outsider because the stranger was to do their gleaning in the corners of the fields only.

The Gentile believers are not considered strangers but rather are considered Abraham's children together with the Jew.

"There is neither Jew nor Greek, (Gentile) there is neither slave nor free, there is neither male nor female; for you are all one in Christ Jesus."

"And if you are Christ's, then you are Abraham's seed, and heirs according to the promise." (Gal. 3: 28-29)

17. So she gleaned in the field until evening, and beat out what she had gleaned, and it was about an ephah of barley."

Beating out what grain you have gathered is called threshing. When a person had a small quantity, as Ruth had, a person used a wooden instrument called a flail. Ruth no doubt used a flail as most likely Gideon used one when he secretly beat out grain.

 "Now the Angel of the LORD came and sat under the terebinth tree which was in Ophrah, which belonged to Joash the Abiezrite, while his son Gideon threshed wheat in the winepress, in order to hide it from the Midianites." (Judges 6:11)

When we listen to, read or watch the word of God being delivered to us whatever we glean from it should be threshed out until we have nothing left but the pure grain. All of men's ideas, interpretations, commentaries, additions, subtractions etc. should all be beaten away that only the pure grain remains. The body of Christ should always utilize a threshing floor.

This is represented in the fact that David purchased Araunah's (Ornan's) threshing floor located on Mt. Moriah the site where Abraham enacted the sacrifice of Isaac.

"Then He said, 'Take now your son, your only son Isaac, whom you love, and go to the land of Moriah, and offer him there as a burnt offering on one of the mountains of which I shall tell you." (Gen 22:2)

David purchased this site and built an altar to the LORD.

" Then Araunah said, 'Why has my lord the king come to his servant' And David said, 'To buy the threshing floor from you, to build an altar to the LORD, that the plague may be withdrawn from the people." (2 Samuel 24:21)

Later Solomon built the first temple or "House of the LORD" on that same site.

"Now Solomon began to build the house of the LORD at Jerusalem on Mount Moriah, where the LORD had appeared to his father David, at the place that David had prepared on the threshing floor of Ornan the Jebusite." (2 Chron. 3:1)

18. Then she took it up and went into the city, and her mother-in-law saw what she had gleaned. So she brought out and gave to her what she had kept back after she had been satisfied."

Ruth exercised the basic principle of loving and giving.

"A new commandment I give to you, that you love one another; as I have loved you, that you also love one another." (John 13:34)

"Heal the sick, cleanse the lepers, raise the dead, cast out demons. Freely you have received, freely give." (Matt 10:8) The grain, in this case barley, represents the word of God.

The Ruth's of the Gentile believers have grown in the things of God so that they are able to share the word they've received from the Lord with their Hebrew brothers and sisters. (The Naomi's)

"And He gave (to the church) some to be apostles, some prophets, some evangelists, and some pastors and teachers"

"for the equipping of the saints (the believers) for the work of the ministry (the believers), for the edifying of the body of Christ," (the believers); all both Jew and Gentile. Eph. 4:11-12)

Not long after the church was established, it fell into the hands of those who wanted to have controlling authority and the word of God was prohibited to what became known as the laity or the people.

Those who turned away and went back to their gods by incorporating them into their "belief system" are the Orpah's of the early church.

The Lord however, made provisions for His true followers, (the Ruth's) and supplied them with enough truth to spiritually feed and sustain them.

"But the woman (church) was given two wings of a great eagle, that she might fly into the wilderness to her place, where she is *nourished* for a time and times and half a time, from the presence of the serpent." (Rev 12:14)

19. **"And her mother-in-law said to her, 'Where have you gleaned today? And where did you work? Blessed be the one who took notice of you'. So she told her mother-in-law with whom she had worked, and said, 'The man's name with whom I worked today is Boaz."**
20. **"Then Naomi said to her daughter-in-law, 'Blessed be he of the LORD, who has not forsaken His kindness to the living and the dead!' And Naomi said to her, 'This man is a relation of ours, one of our close relatives."**

Naomi immediately recognized that favor had been given to Ruth for the abundance of grain she returned with. Once hearing whose field Ruth had worked in Naomi knew the LORD had his hand in it.

When the early Christians who were all Jews learned that the Gentiles, had accepted the Messiah they rejoiced.

"When they heard these things, they became silent; and they glorified God, saying, 'Then God has also granted to the Gentiles repentance to life." (Acts 11:18)

21. **"Ruth the Moabitess said, 'He also said to me, 'You shall stay close by my young men until they have finished all my harvest."**
22. **"And Naomi said to Ruth her daughter-in-law, 'It is good, my daughter, that you go out with his young women, and that people do not meet you in any other field."**

23. "So she stayed close by the young women of Boaz, to glean until the end of barley harvest and wheat harvest; and she dwelt with her mother-in-law."

Once Christ has given us of His grace and we have eaten from His table His precious word from His own hand, we should never be found laboring in any man's field but His.

As Ruth stayed close by the young women laboring in Boaz's field, the early Gentile church stayed close by the young Jewish churches laboring in the Lord's field. The Gentile church was spiritually close and bonded to the Jerusalem assemblies and had a love and dedication to their wellbeing.

"Now concerning the collection for the saints, as I have given orders to the churches of Galatia, so you must do also:"

"On the first day of the week let each one of you lay something aside, storing up as he may prosper; that there be no collections when I come."

"And when I come, whomever you approve by your letters I will send to bear your gift to Jerusalem." (1 Cor 16: 1-3)

Regarding the collection on the "first day of the week", they went by the Hebrew week. The first day begin at sundown after the Sabbath or our Saturday. They set aside Saturday dedicated to God according to the 4th commandment.

Constantine despised the Jews with a hatred and vengeance as they did not commit to his religious ruling. Thus, anything that pertained to Jewish manner of worship became forbidden and because he was a "son god" worshipper. (A popular Roman coin had the image of the sun god Mithra, on the back of the coin and on the front was Constantine's image. The words sol Invictus meaning the unconquered sun was also on the coins.)

Constantine gave an edict that changed the day of worship from Saturday to Sunday March 7, 321 C.E. The following are the words he wrote translated into the English language.

"On the venerable day of the sun let the magistrate and people residing in cities rest, and let all workshops be closed. In the country however, persons engaged in agricultural work may freely and lawfully continue their pursuits; because it often happens that another day is not s suitable for grain growing or for vine planting; lest by neglecting the proper moment for such operations the bounty of heaven should be lost." (Schaffs History of the Christian Church, vol. III, chap. 75)

Once that became law then anyone found worshipping on a Saturday was penalized financially or by other means. Sometimes the penalties were severe and physical. It did not take long for people to tolerate and submit to the new approach in Christianity.

THE BOOK OF RUTH

CHAPTER 3

1. **"Then Naomi her mother-in-law said to her, 'My daughter, shall I not seek security for you, that it may be well with you?"**
2. **"Now Boaz, whose young women you were with, is he not our relative? In fact, he is winnowing barley tonight at the threshing floor."**
3. **"Therefore wash yourself and anoint yourself, put on your best garment and go down to the threshing floor; but do not make yourself known to the man until he has finished eating and drinking."**

Naomi considers Ruth close family. She calls Ruth her daughter and in referring to Boaz she uses the words "our relative", not my relative.

Likewise, the Gentile church is a daughter to the Jerusalem above. The Jews, being of the region of Judea are biologically close relatives to the Messiah or Christ. Through the redemptive, cleansing power of His shed blood we are made one with them in Christ.

"But now in Christ Jesus you who once were far off have been brought near by the blood of Christ" (Eph 2:13)

"For it pleased the Father that in Him all the fullness should dwell,"

33

"and by Him to reconcile all things to Himself, by Him, whether things on earth or things in heaven, having made peace through the blood of His cross." (Col 1:19-20)

Naomi gives instruction to Ruth to wash and attire herself in her best garment before going to meet Boaz at the threshing floor where he is winnowing the barley.

And in a like manner, the apostles with other Hebrew believers of the early church were eager to assist and instruct the Gentiles in preparation of becoming a bride to the Messiah. Similarly, we are to cleanse ourselves of sin and put on the garment of righteousness and make ourselves ready to meet our redeemer.

"Let us be glad and rejoice and give Him glory, for the marriage of the Lamb has come, and His wife has made herself ready."

"And to her it was granted to be arrayed in fine linen, clean and bright, for the fine linen is the righteous acts of the saints." (Rev 19:7-8)

"Husbands, love your wives, just as Christ also loved the church an gave Himself for her"

"that He might sanctify and cleanse her with the washing of water by the word,"

"That He might present her to Himself a glorious church, not having spot or wrinkle or any such thing, but that she should be holy and without blemish." (Eph 5:25-27)

Ruth will meet Boaz at the threshing floor. We also meet Christ at the threshing floor for we are threshing out false doctrine from our hearts and replacing it with His pure word. And he will purge His floor with us, separating the wheat from the chaff. Whatever is not good grain or truth, will be blown away and ultimately consumed.

"And in their mouth was found no deceit, (lie) for they are without fault before the throne of God." (Rev 14:5)

4. "Then it shall be, when he lies down, that you shall notice the place where he lies; and you shall go in, uncover his feet, and lie down; and he will tell you what you should do."

5. "And she said to her, 'All that you say to me I will do."

6. "So she went down to the threshing floor and did according to all that her mother-in-law instructed her."

7. "And after Boaz had eaten and drunk, and his heart was cheerful, he went to lie down at the end of the heap of grain; and she came softly, uncovered his feet, and lay down."

Ruth was careful and quiet so as not to awaken Boaz but, to allow him to sleep undisturbed.

"I charge you, O daughters of Jerusalem, Do not stir up nor awaken love until it pleases."   (Song of Solomon 8:4)

8. "Now it happened at midnight that the man was startled, and turned himself; and there, a woman was lying at his feet."

This shadow of events particularly stirs my spirit because to me, it is so beautiful. Ruth is portraying that part of the Gentile believer who sold themselves out to become a child of Abraham. Boaz is a type of Christ. She, the church, has become a close relative to Christ by the receiving of the Holy Spirit. She humbles herself at the feet of Christ and lays her burdens down. She proposes to Him (take your maidservant under your wing) declaring that she wants to be chosen and numbered as His bride. (Some versions say spread your skirt over me however, it is more correct to say wing because it is referring to the wing of his shawl.)

9. "And he said, 'Who are you?' So she answered, 'I am Ruth, your maidservant. Take your maidservant under your wing, for you are a close relative."

10. "Then he said, 'Blessed are you of the LORD, my daughter! For you have shown more kindness at the end than at the

beginning, in that you did not go after young men, whether poor or rich."

Boaz calls her blessed of the LORD because she showed more kindness at the end than at the beginning, in that she didn't go after young men, whether poor or rich.

In the beginning would be the beginning of the "Gentile church", when many of those believers turned back to their idols (young men whether poor or rich: some nations religions were very rich, i.e., the Egyptian gods) But the Ruth's of the church remained and kept their loyalty to the true God the God of Abraham.

The humbleness, meekness and willingness to lay yourself down before the Lord and present yourself to Him as a living sacrifice is the spirit of the Gentile bride members.

She is at the threshing floor which holds great significance to the believer for it was on Ornan's threshing floor that David had purchased, on Mt. Moriah that Solomon built the temple, and also the same Mt. Moriah our Lord was crucified on.

"Now Solomon began to build the house of the LORD at Jerusalem on Mount Moriah, where the LORD had appeared to his father David, at the place that David had prepared on the threshing floor of Ornan the Jebusite." (2Chron 3:1)

The feet in the word of God represent your understanding.

The Hebrew word for thresh is: duwsh, doosh-or dowsh, dosh; or diysh, deesh; a primitive root; to trample or thresh: -break, tear, thresh, tread out (down), at grass (Jer. 50:11, by mistake for; deshe' (H1877)

There are many pastors who say that Boaz was surprised to see a "woman" at the threshing floor because women were not allowed at the threshing floor. This is a misconception. History teaches us that women frequently were at the threshing floor helping to thresh grain. Also, one of their primary jobs was that of sifting it after it was threshed. In this process any left-over chaff or other unwanted materials such as a small stone, would be removed. Christ's church does the same with the word delivered to them. They sift through and remove any false doctrines, idolatries or misconceptions preached or taught. Much like the Berean's did in Paul's day.

All the work to prepare and make the grain suitable for use was shared as befitting for the need. In ancient times a flail was used for small quantities. Ruth probably used one to beat out the barley she'd gleaned. (Ruth 2:17)

And Gideon probably used a flail when he was hiding from the Midianites and pretending to beat out the wheat in the winepress. (Judges 6:11

There was a threshing tool used made of two wooden planks, about three feet wide and six feet long, joined together with rows of square holes cut under them to hold stones or pieces of sharp metal.

"Behold I will make you into a new threshing sledge with sharp teeth; you shall thresh the mountains and beat them small, and make the hills like chaff." (Isa 41:15)

This threshing sledge was pulled by oxen. Oxen in ancient Israel are not necessarily bulls. Rather they are bovine either male or female. The Oxen pulled the sledge over the grain and the person threshing stood or set on the sledge with a goad in hand to prod a slow Oxen along.

"For the black cumin is not threshed with a threshing sledge, nor is a cart- wheel rolled over the cumin; but the black cumin is beaten out with a stick, and the cumin with a rod."

"Bread flour must be ground; Therefore he does not thresh it forever, break it with his cartwheel, or crush it with his horsemen. (Isa 28:27-28)

The "cartwheel" was a wagon or cart that had cylinder shaped wheels under it and was generally drawn by oxen.

The most favored method of threshing by the ancient Israelites was the use of oxen driven over the grain, allowing their hoofs to do the work because as they walked over the grain, they would both turn it over and crush it.

The oxen were not muzzled while threshing, but were allowed to eat their portion as they treaded over the grain. and even today the Arab farmers won't muzzle their oxen believing it would be sinful to do so.

"You shall not muzzle an ox while it treads out the grain." (Deut.25:4)

"Whoever goes to war at his own expense? Who plants a vineyard and does not eat of its fruit? Or who tends a flock and does not drink of the milk of the flock?"

"Do I say these things as mere man? Or does not the law say the same also?"

"For it is written in the law of Moses, 'You shall not muzzle an ox while it treads out the grain.' Is it oxen God is concerned about?"

"Or does He say it altogether for our sakes? For our sakes, no doubt, this is written, that he who plows should plow in hope, and he who threshes in hope should be partaker of his hope." (1 Cor. 9: 7-10)

Boaz was winnowing that evening. Winnowing was accomplished with a bent pronged fork made of wood or a wide shovel. The grain along with the chaff and straw was thrown against the wind and because the grain was heaviest it would fall to the ground while the straw would land in a heap off to the side. But the chaff being light of any substance would blow further into a windrow.

"His winnowing fan is in His hand, and He will thoroughly clean out His threshing floor, and gather His wheat into the barn; but He will burn up the chaff with unquenchable fire." (Matt 3:12)

11. "And now, my daughter, do not fear. I will do for you all that you request, for all the people of my town know that you are a virtuous woman"

12. "Now it is true that I am a close relative; however, here is a relative closer than I."

13. "Stay this night, and in the morning, it shall be that if he will perform the duty of a close relative for you-good; let him do it. But if he does not want to perform the duty for you, as the LORD lives! Lie down until morning."

14. "So she lay at his feet until morning, and she arose before one could recognize another. Then he said, 'Do not let it be known that the woman came to the threshing floor."

15. "Also he said, 'Bring the shawl that is on you and hold it.' And when she held it, he measured six ephahs of barley, and laid it on her. Then she went into the city."

When we come to the Lord and lay ourselves down at His feet and present to him an open honest heart declaring, I am your friend, your servant, take me under your wing, make me your bride, He receives, comforts and assures us that we will belong to Him that He will redeem us.

Stay through the night or until the morning suggests: Continue to lay yourself at the foot of the cross through the dark times and keep your trust in Him.

Since the church began there has been dark periods of persecutions, false doctrine, confusions and fears. The Lord knew that there would be spiritual darkness over the earth.

"I must work while it is day; the night is coming when no one can work."

"As long as I am in the world, I am the light of the world." (John 9:4-5)

"Are there not twelve hours in the day? If anyone walks in the day, he does not stumble, because he sees the light of this world."

"But if one walks in the night, he stumbles, because the light is not in him." (John 11:9-10)

The apostles warned the assemblies of the darkness that was approaching.

"Therefore take heed to yourselves and to all the flock, among which the Holy Spirit has made you overseers, to shepherd the church of God which He purchased with His own blood."

"For I know this, that after my departure savage wolves will come in among you, not sparing the flock."

"Also from among yourselves men will rise up, speaking perverse things, to draw away the disciples after themselves."

"Therefore watch and remember that for three years I did not cease to warn everyone night and day with tears." (Acts 20:28-31)

It may appear dark now but look up for your redemption draws nigh.

Boaz lay six ephahs of barley on her. This is a picture of Christ imparting the word of God, which covers six thousand years given to mankind, to His church and when the millennial day (seventh thousandth year) begins to dawn we start our journey to the city; the "new Jerusalem".

16. **"When she came to her mother-in-law, she said, 'Is that you, my daughter?' Then she told her all that the man had done for her."**

17. **"And she said, 'These six ephahs of barley he gave me; for he said to me, 'Do not go empty handed to your mother-in-law."**

18. **"Then she said, 'Sit still, my daughter, until you know how the matter will turn out; for the man will not rest until he has concluded the matter this day."**

The Gentle church will not be empty handed. They will be able to present God's word in its fullness and truth. And the Lord will not rest until He has accomplished what He set out to do.

"Being confident of this very thing, that He who has begun a good work in you will complete it until the day of Jesus Christ;" (Phil 1:6)

THE BOOK OF RUTH
CHAPTER 4

1. "Now Boaz went up to the gate and sat down there; and behold, the close relative of whom Boaz had spoken came by. So Boaz said, 'Come aside, friend, sit down here.' So he came aside and sat down."

2. "And he took ten men of the elders of the city, and said, 'Sit down here.' So they sat down."

3. And then he said to the close relative, Naomi, who has come back from the country of Moab, sold the piece of land which belonged to our brother Elimelech."

4. "And I thought to inform you, saying, 'Buy it back in the presence of the inhabitants and the elders of my people. If you will redeem it, redeem it; but if you will not redeem it, then tell me, that I may know; for there is no one but you to redeem it, and I am next after you.' And he said, 'I will redeem it."

5. "Then Boaz said, 'On the day you buy the field from the hand of Naomi, you must also buy it from Ruth the Moabitess, the wife of the dead, to perpetuate the name of the dead through his inheritance."

6. **"And the close relative said, 'I cannot redeem it for myself, lest I ruin my own inheritance. You redeem my right of redemption for yourself, for I cannot redeem it."**

This "close" relative is a type of the unbelieving Jew. The religious element of Israel the Pharisees, Scribes, Sadducees, Essenes or the Judeans in general.

They were given the opportunity to buy the field, in fact, they were given forty years to redeem the field and not lose it. They were blind to the treasure that was there for them.

Jesus had been crucified in the approximate year of 30 C.E. and Jerusalem remained until approximately 70 C.E. Thus, they had forty years to hear the gospel and accept Jesus as the Messiah of Israel and His church which included the Gentiles.

"Again, the kingdom of heaven is like treasure hidden in a field, which a man found and hid; and for joy over it he goes and sells all that he has and buys that field." (Matt 13:44)

The relative first considers the purchase but as soon as he learns that there is a "woman" that is a part of the bargain, he suddenly fears he'd lose his own inheritance.

The Judeans had no problem in taking the inheritance of the Jews. But those who were Christians or who followed the Way, as it was then called, would be rejected. They wanted nothing to do with the woman.

They began persecuting them and trying to eliminate them from their land. However, they could not advance on the Gentile element of the church as the people belonged to the nations around them. None – the – less, the entire church soon suffered persecution under Rome. The Judaeans wanted to snuff out their brethren of the Way because they preached the gospel of Jesus and there were signs such as healings among them which they considered to be a threat. So, to the Judeans this was the same threat as Christ was to their position with Rome whom they provisionally relied on. Also, they were giving honor to another king besides Caesar and in the mind of the Judean, they were disobedient to the laws of the land.

"Then the chief priests and the Pharisees gathered a council and said, 'What shall we do? For this Man works many signs."

"If we let Him alone like this, everyone will believe in Him, and the Romans will come and take away both our place and nation." (John 11: 47 - 48)

In this field, truth is sown. Truth was sown by Christ and then by His apostles and by His church truth continued to be sown. These truths are a priceless treasure and His church is a righteous woman and a part of the treasure.

"Who can find a virtuous wife? For her worth is far above rubies" (Prov 31:10)

7. **"Now this was the custom in former times in Israel concerning redeeming and exchanging, to confirm anything: one man took off his sandal and gave it to the other and this was a confirmation in Israel."**
8. **"Therefore the close relative said to Boaz, 'Buy it for yourself.' So he took off his sandal."**
9. **"And Boaz said to the elders and all the people, 'You are witnesses this day that I have bought all that was Elimelech's, and all that was Chilion's and Mahlon's, from the hand of Naomi"**
10. **"Moreover, Ruth the Moabitess, the widow of Mahlon, I have acquired as my wife, to perpetuate the name of the dead through his inheritance, that the name of the dead may not be cut off from among his brethren and from his position at the gate. You are witnesses this day"**

The idea of removing a shoe and giving it as confirmation was in effect saying that the walk or direction we are taking is guaranteed. Should I change my direction then you may bring the shoe to me as evidence of our agreement.

Your feet represent your understanding which designates the direction, way or path you walk in life or in your faith.

In bible times the shoe being the attire of the feet, was held as significance to the understanding or direction, one took. It was one's walk in life.

"Now Moses was tending the flock of Jethro his father-in-law, the priest of Midian. And he led the flock to the back of the desert, and came to Horeb, the mountain of God."

"And the Angel of the LORD appeared to him in a flame of fire from the midst of a bush. So he looked, an behold, the bush was burning with fire, but the bush was not consumed."

Then Moses said, 'I will now turn aside and see this great sight, why the bush does not burn."

"So when the LORD saw that he turned aside to look, God called to him from the midst of the bush and said, 'Moses, Moses!' And he said 'Here I am."

The He said, 'Do not draw near this place. Take your sandals off your feet, for the place where you stand is holy ground." (Ex 3:1-5)

Take off your understanding, your way. You cannot stand on Holy places before the Lord while you are standing on your own understanding, your own ways or the ways of the world, or false religion.

"Trust in the LORD with all your heart and lean not on your own understanding." (Prov 3:5)

Everyone primarily walked to their destination. They were walking through dirt, mud and at times unpleasant things as well. The shoe could become filthy with the way a person walked.

"Gilead is Mine, and Manasseh is Mine; Ephraim also is the helmet for My head; Judah is My lawgiver,"

"Moab is My washpot; Over Edom I will cast My shoe; Philistia, shout in triumph because of Me." (Ps 60:7-8

"John answered them, saying, I baptize with water, but there stands One among you whom you do not know."

"It is He who coming after me, is preferred before me, whose sandal strap I am not worthy to lose." (John 1:26-27)

When a guest came into a home, the servant of the house would unlatch and remove the guest's shoes and wash their feet from the debris they collected on their journey over. John was so humble he said he wasn't even worthy to do this menial labor for Christ.

A person's shoes would get extremely dusty as there were no paved roads to travel on nor concrete sidewalks. Their feet would sweat and literally create a mud on their feet.

"Jesus, knowing that the Father had given all things into His hands, and that He had come from God and was going to God, "

"rose from supper and laid aside His garments, took a towel and girded Himself."

"After that, He poured water into a basin and began to wash the disciples' feet, and to wipe them with the towel with which He was girded." (John 13:3-5)

Jesus gave a beautiful example of how we are to humble ourselves and treat one another.

"And whoever will not receive you nor hear your words, when you depart from that house or city, shake off the dust from your feet."

"Assuredly, I say to you, it will be more tolerable for the land of Sodom and Gomorrah in the day of judgment that for that city!" (Math 10:14-15)

The shaking off of the dust was a display of disgust and depicted how they would not at that point, have any part with them. It equates with Ps 60:8 where the LORD said he'd cast his shoe over Edom.

11. **"And all the people were at the gate, and the elders said, 'We are witnesses. The LORD make the woman who is coming to your house like Rachel and Leah, the two who built the house of Israel, and may you prosper in Ephrathah and be famous in Bethlehem."**

12. **"May your house be like the house of Perez, whom Tamar bore to Judah, because of the offspring which the LORD will give you from this young woman."**

This statement that the elders made was a prophetic statement. Tamar in the book of Genesis, was also a Gentile; a Canaanite woman. In Geneses 38, Judah departed from his brethren. He finds a woman whom he marries.

"It came to pass at that time that Judah departed from his brothers, and visited a certain Adullamite whose name was Hirah."

"And Judah saw there a daughter of a certain Canaanite whose name was Shua, and he married her and went in to her."

"So she conceived and bore a son, and he called his name Er."

"She conceived again and bore a son and she called his name Onan."

"And she conceived yet again and bore a son, and called his name Shelah, he was a Chezib when she bore him." (Gen 38: 1-5)

The name Chezib may be from the name Achzib, a town that rested in the lowlands. The name interestingly means deceitful while the name Shelah refers closely meaning to send; depart; send away or petition.

The name Er is referenced in meaning as a "wild ass" which apparently fit his character.

"Then Judah took a wife for Er his firstborn, and her name was Tamar."

"But Er, Judah's firstborn, was wicked in the sight of the LORD, and the LORD killed him."

"And Judah said to Onan, 'Go in to your brother's wife and marry her, and raise up an heir to your brother.'"

"But Onan knew that the heir would not be his; and it came to pass, when he went in to his brother's wife, that he emitted on the ground, lest he should give an heir to his brother."

"And the thing which he did displeased the LORD; therefore He killed him."

"Then Judah said to Tamar his daughter-in-law, 'Remain a widow in your father's house until my son Shelah is grown,' For he said,' Lest he also die like his bothers,' And Tamar went and dwelt in her father's house."

"Now in the process of time the daughter of Shua, Judah's wife, died, and Judah was comforted, and went up to his sheepshearers at Timnah, he and his friend Hirah the Adullamite." (Gen38 6-12)

What we are seeing here is the gracious mercy of the LORD. Judah's behavior was corrupt in all of this. He left his brethren and married a Canaanite woman. He made a promise to his daughter-in-law then back tracked by leaving her in her aging widowhood. Yet the LORD used Judah to bring forth the Messiah of Israel and savior of the world.

"The scepter shall not depart from Judah, nor a lawgiver from between his feet, until Shiloh comes; And to Him shall be the obedience of the people." (Gen 49: 10)

"And it was told Tamar, saying, 'Look, your father-in-law is going up to Timnah, to shear his sheep."

"So she took off her widows' garments, covered herself with a veil and wrapped herself, and sat in an open place which was on the way to Timnah; for she saw that Shelah was grown, and she was not given to him to wife."

"When Judah saw her, he thought she was a harlot, because she had covered her face."

"Then he turned to her by the way, and said, 'Please let me come in to you'; for he did not know that she was his daughter-in-law. So she said, 'What will you give me?'

"And he said, 'I will send a young goat from the flock.' So she said, 'Will you give me a pledge till you send it?"

"Then he said, 'What pledge shall I give you?' So she said, 'Your signet and cord, and your staff that is in your hand.' Then he gave them to her, and went in to her, and she conceived by him" (Gen 38:13-18)

Tamar must have known her father-in-law well. She knew he would be easily seduced and played a prostitute. Having children was of the upmost importance for women during that period of time. She had spent years waiting for the promise that Judah broke. She was not going to go childless because of Judah's lack of integrity.

Judah did keep his word and sent by his servant the goat he had promised but, the servant retuned with the goat when he couldn't fine her as she had changed back into her former attire and left the place she had been seated.

"Then Judah said, 'Let her take them for herself, lest we be shamed; for I sent this young goat and you have not found her."

"And it came to pass, about three months after, that Judah was told, saying, 'Tamar your daughter-in-law has played the harlot; furthermore, she is with child by harlotry.' So Judah said, 'Bring her out and let her be burned!" (Gen 38: 23-24)

How sardonic and biased is this? Judah is going to have Tamar "burned" for an act that he himself participated in. Not to mention the innocent baby she's carrying.

"When she was brought out, she sent to her father-in-law, saying, 'By the man to whom these belong, I am with child'. And she said, 'Please determine who's these are-the signet and cord, and staff."

"So Judah acknowledged them and said, 'She has been more righteous than I, because I did not give her to Shelah my son.' And he never knew her again.

Here Judah displays his integrity as he acknowledges not only his belongings but, more importantly, he acknowledges his fault and humbles himself to what is right.

"Now it came to pass, at the time for giving birth, that behold, twins were in her womb."

"And so it was, when she was giving birth, that the one put out his hand; and the midwife took a scarlet thread and bound it on his hand, saying, 'This one came out first."

"Then it happened, as he drew back his hand, that his brother came out unexpectedly; and she said, 'How did you break through? This breach be upon you'! Therefore his name was called Perez."

"Afterward his brother came out who had the scarlet thread on his hand. And his name was called Zerah." (Gen 38: 25-30)

Tamar and Perez are both in the lineage of Christ and both listed in the gospel of Mathew, Mary's lineage. And Perez in the gospel of Luke, Mary's husband Joseph's lineage.

"Abraham begot Isaac, Isaac begot Judah and his brothers,"

Judah begot Perez and Zerah by Tamar, Perez begot Hezron, and Hezron begot Ram." (Math 1: 2-3) "the son of Aminadab, the son of Ram, the son of Hezron the son of Perez, the son of Judah," (Luke 3:33)

13. "so Boaz took Ruth and she became his wife, and when he went in to her, the LORD gave her conception, and she bore a son."

14. "Then the women said to Naomi, 'Blessed be the LORD, who has not left you this day without a close relative, and may his name be famous in Israel!"

15. "And may he be to you a restorer of life and nourisher of your old age; for your daughter-in-law, who loves you, who is better to you than seven sons, has born him." (Ruth 4: 13-15)

Remarkably, both statements made in verse 12 by the men and verse 14 & 15 by the women are prophetically precise. The offspring that Ruth contributed became the seed (Christ) and descendants (heirs) of Abraham. The statement that Ruth, was better to Naomi than "SEVEN SON'S". is packed with prophetic interpretation. It actually implies that Jerusalem's inherited Gentile daughter-in-law (the Ruth part of the Gentile Church) is better to her than ALL of Israel has been. The number seven meaning complete (all) and son's is generally referencing to children but, in this case, it is referencing to the builder of a family name (Strong's H 1121; Ben} and refers to the male. Interestingly however, it's root comes from Strong's H 1129; Bana which is what God did when He took the rib of Adam and "built" the woman.

"Then the rib which the LORD God had taken from man He – **made - H1129** into a woman, and He brought her to the man." (Gen. 2: 22)

16. "Then Naomi took the child and laid him on her bosom, and became a nurse to him."

I have heard individuals speculate that Naomi breast-fed the child because of the way this sentence reads. However, the word bosom is the

Hebrew word **cheyq** which means to in close, bosom, lap, midst, within. We would say to hold or embrace. The word nurse in this sentence is the Hebrew word **aman** which means to build up or support; foster as a parent or nurse. So, she simply took him in her arms and became as any grandmother would become to their grandchild. Loving, caring and supportive.

17. **"Also the neighbor women gave him a name, saying, 'There is a son born to Naomi.' And they called his name Obed. He is the father of Jesse, the father of David."**
18. **"Now this is the genealogy of Perez: Perez begot Hezron;"**
19. **"Hezron begot Ram, and Ram begot Amminadab;"**
20. **"Amminadab begot Nahshon, and Nahshon begot Salmon;"**
21. **"Salmon begot Boaz, and Boaz begot Obed;"**
22. **"Obed begot Jesse, and Jesse begot David."**

At this point, we close the pages to the book of Ruth however, the story continues on. Although Ruth is one of the shortest books in the bible it is one of the most treasured and instructional books. Packed with many other stories, types and shadows. Indeed, the book was finished yet, the story carries on. Not just in the telling of the story rather, it is carried on in our lives. Our approach to God, His word and His people.

The Book of Ruth conveys to the reader a choice. A large portion of the early church turned away from its mother, from Jerusalem above, and went back to its familiar home grounds. They chose to go back to their familiar gods by incorporating them into the church and took on new husbands, or heads over assemblies, districts etc. They incorporated their pagan religious celebrations by making them "Christin" holidays. They became the Oprah's of the called out.

A remnant however, remained faithful to the Father and continued in the provender of truth foraged and dispensed by the mother they clung to, the church that Christ built, the Jerusalem above. These are the Ruth's who have remained with the early believers hidden in Christ and will rise again to reign with Him a thousand years. They died out to their former self and their former ways, they truly repented, that is turned from their own ways and took on that of Christ.

"For you died, and your life is hidden with Christ in God."

"When Christ who is our life appears, then you also will appear with Him in glory." (Colossians 3: 3-4)

It is important to note in reading about Boaz and his field that Ruth worked in, that there were other fields throughout Judah and even Bethlehem. Boaz's field was one of many throughout the region. This world has many fields to work in. Many religions and many beliefs. But, just as there is only one way, and that is through Christ Jesus, there is only one field where the treasure is hidden. We want to be working in that field and gather in the best that God has to offer.

We want to leave this world behind, sell out to this world and all that is in it and buy that field.

"Again the kingdom of heaven is like a treasure hidden in a field, which a man found and hid, and for joy over it he goes and sells all that he has and buys that field." (Mathew 13:44)

This is all the work of our Father. His great plan of salvation.

Our heavenly Father is amazing. The word pictures He has painted for us coming from real life events in order to instruct us in His ways and open our understanding to the depth of His love toward us is absolutely astounding.

We that believe in the redemptive power of Christ the Messiah, should endeavor to be like Ruth whether Gentile or Jew her Spirit should be carboned within us.

Let us like Ruth, go forward with the Naomi's and hold tight to her God For we have been brought to the house of bread where we are nourished unto all eternity. And being nourished let us grow into the fulness and stature of Christ so that we may be presented to our Heavenly Father. Redeemed by the owner of the field even Yeshua Messiah, Jesus Christ the only begotten of the Father and savior of the world, to Him be Glory and Power forever and ever Amen!

Bethlehem and surrounding areas.

Ruth declares her love for her mother-in-law Naomi, engraving by Gustave Dore (1832-1883), from The Holy Scriptures containing the Old and New Testaments: Translated from The Latin Vulgate by Antonio Martini (1721-1809), with friezes by Enrico Giacomelli, Ruth 1, 14, Volume 1, 1869-1870 edition.

Preparing sheaves to bring to the **threshing floor**

Traditional threshing with a threshing board in the **Near East**

Engraved tablet from **Kish**, dating from **3350 BC,** with representations of threshing boards on both sides

Antique illustration - from Harper's Monthly Vol 60 1880

1628 moeyaert- Ruth and Boaz

Alchimowicz-44